Arise
and
Declare
the Word!

Arise and Declare the Word!

Deborah L. Grant

Unlock Publishing House, Inc.

Unlock Publishing House
6715 Suitland Road Suite A
Morningside MD 20746
www.unlockpublishinghouse.com
1(301)420-2077

ISBN: 978-0-9838982-9-0

Editing by Maletta Pritchett

DEDICATION

I dedicate this book to my brothers and sisters in Christ who dare to go after everything that God has for you!

Also to my brother Darris and brother in law Derrick: Again I say to you both, "it's not over until YOU win and with God all things are possible to them that believe!"

ACKNOWLEDGEMENTS

To my best friend, my Lord and Savior Jesus Christ, whom I love and wholeheartedly serve! Thank you for loving me and calling me into the kingdom for such a time as this! I won't let you down!

Secondly, my husband of 17 years and closest friend Donald: I love and adore you! The best is yet to come for us! To our beautiful children, Jada (which means a jewel), Donovan (which means leader and ruler), and Nia Joy (which means purpose and jubilance): I love and treasure you all! You are the generation of the upright and you are blessed!

To my mom (Nanny): You're my sweetie! Thank you for introducing me to Christ and training me up in the way I should go, always keeping me around the word.

My pastors, Dr.'s Mike and Dee Dee Freeman of Spirit of Faith Christian Center: Thank you for pouring into my life the spirit of faith! I got it! Much love!

Thank you Pastors Dewayne and Lisa freeman for your example of meekness and love and encouragement!

Minister Rachel Langston, Natasha Cherry, and Aisha Davis for all your hard work and assistance with this book! I love and appreciate you all! I'm writing the next one so be ready!

CONTENTS

> **Isaiah 60:1** "Arise, shine, for your light has come, and the glory of the LORD rises upon you."

Arise and Declare the Word!

Arise ~ A physical change of position.

Declare ~ To announce, report or to proclaim.

The Word ~ The message from the Lord delivered with

His authority and made effective by His power.

(Vines Expository Dictionary)

INTRODUCTION

Do you have dreams and aspirations to live the good life and to be a blessing to others? Well, even if you don't at this present time, I have good news for you! The abundant life that God has predestined for you to experience and enjoy is waiting for you to realize it, and then seize it! He said in His word, "beloved I wish above ALL things that thou mayest prosper and be in health even as thy soul prospers." This is God's desire; but in order to apprehend what He has reserved for us, we have to arise and pursue it with passion!

This book was written primarily for the purpose of causing a change to take place in your thinking relative to how you presently see yourself, and to cause a transformation of your mind on how God sees you. This book was also written to cause a new boldness to exude from within as you declare the promises of God to come to fruition in your daily life. The word says that "the kingdom of heaven suffers violence and the violent take it by force!" How bad do you want your dreams and God-ordained destiny? You have to take it! Opportunity in most cases does not knock; it sits there quietly waiting to be realized!

The title of this book "Arise and Declare the Word" was given to me specifically, to clearly define the shift that must take place in our speaking, thinking and believing. The word arise means to change your posture and position. We've been wrongly positioned in our thinking for far too long. We have not understood that when we pray, we are not trying to get God to please do something! He is the One who prompts us, by His spirit, to pray and act on His word. He desires to accomplish some things in the earth.

You and I are the ones who are here to do business on his behalf. To declare the word in faith is a part of acting on the word. Faith without works or action is dead, which really means it is inoperable. It won't produce anything to say I have faith, but have no corresponding action to get what you have faith in! Philippians 2:13 says, "For it is God that works in you, both to will and to do his good pleasure".

He wants us to arise. Don't just sit there complaining, worrying, crying, and hoping something good will come out of a bad situation. No, arise; change your posture and your position! Hold your head up, square your shoulders, renew your mind, get full of what He has said about you, and boldly declare the word! Declare means to make a formal announcement. What are we announcing? We are announcing that the promises of God, which is the will of God, is the truth about our situation and not the present facts that we see temporarily! This book will teach you how to do this with power, authority and confidence. Your speech will change! Your thinking will change! How you see yourself will change! Your believing and acting on the word will change! Ultimately your life will change for the better! If you're ready for a radical change to take place in your life, then keep on reading. If you want to see Gods' original intent concerning you, then adopt and put into practice the principles that are presented in the following chapters. How bad do you want it? Let's Arise and declare the infallible word of our God!

> **1John 3:2** "Beloved, now are we the sons of God…" (AKJV)

1

Know Who You Are

We are not a people without relationship or covenant. We entered into a covenant relationship with God when we accepted Jesus Christ as our Lord and Savior. As heirs of that covenant, there are many wonderful promises that we are entitled to (Galatians 3:29). 2 Peter 1:4 lets us know this: "Whereby are given to us exceeding great and precious promises: that by these you might be partakers of the divine nature…" This is why we must become aware of our relationship with our heavenly Father; in order to claim and protect what rightfully belongs to us as heirs.

We do not have to try to convince God to do something for us. The Word of God says in 2 Peter 1:3 that He has already given us all things that pertain to or are necessary for life and godliness. He has given us all things richly to enjoy. Even though it is His good pleasure to give us the Kingdom and to supply all of our needs, if we do not understand our relationship and position with the Father, we will leave all of His promises unclaimed.

Revelation 19:16 says that He (God) is the King of Kings and the Lord of Lords. It also says in 1 Peter 2:9, "you are a chosen generation, a royal priesthood, an holy nation, a peculiar people; that you should show forth the praises of him who has called you out of darkness into his marvelous light." You and I are kings and priests unto the Lord and as such, when we speak, our words have authority and carry much weight. Heaven and earth respond to spoken words even as they responded in the book of Genesis, chapter 1.

> v. 3 And God said, "Let there be light," and there was light.
> v. 6-7 And God said, "Let there be an expanse between the waters to separate water from water." So God made the expanse and separated the water under the expanse from the water above it. And it was so.
> v. 9 And God said, "Let the water under the sky be gathered to one place, and let dry ground appear." And it was so.
> v. 11 Then God said, "Let the land produce vegetation: seed-bearing plants and trees on the land that bear fruit with seed in it, according to their various kinds." And it was so.
> v. 14-15 And God said, "Let there be lights in the expanse of the sky to separate the day from the night, and let them serve as signs to mark seasons and days and years, and let them be lights in the expanse of the sky to give light on the earth." And it was so
> v. 24 God said, "Let the land produce living creatures

according to their kinds: livestock, creatures that move along the ground, and wild animals, each according to its kind." And it was so.

Take note that everything God spoke materialized and came into existence. Verse 27 of this same chapter lets us know that mankind was created in the image of God; meaning we were created in His very likeness. Just as His words carry authority and have creative power, so do our words since we have been created in His very image and likeness. "As He is" (the Lord Jesus Christ), "so are we in this world (I John 4:17)." When you truly understand who you are (son of God, king and priest), it will radically change the way you see and carry yourself, view your circumstances, and navigate through life. Your speech will change, you'll talk differently, and you will begin to lay hold of your inheritance and possess what the word says is already yours.

ARISE

> **Isaiah 43:26** "Put me in remembrance: *let us* plead together: declare you, that you may be justified" (AKJV)

2

Agree With God

We have to take possession of the promises of God. We do so by agreeing with God's Word for our situation. This involves finding a scriptural promise and declaring it in faith. In Isaiah 43:26, God said, "Put me in remembrance: let us plead together: declare thou, that you may be justified."

Agreeing with God means that you will say and believe what He has promised in His Word. It means that His vocabulary will become your vocabulary. You must allow His words to fill your mouth, be spoken in faith, and release them to work in your life. Colossians 3:16 says, "Let the word of Christ dwell in you richly in all wisdom…" Retrain yourself to respond in every situation with the word of God, regardless of how you feel, what you see, or what others may think. When you agree with God, you settle in your heart that His truth is greater than any present fact that may exist. 2 Corinthians 4:18 says, "...we look not at the things which are seen, [because they are temporal] but at the things which are not seen: [because they] are eternal."

My children often get in the car and say, "Mom, you can't be listening to this again! I'm starting to remember everything its saying!" I think to myself ... Exactly! Faith doesn't come by what you have heard. No, faith comes by continuously hearing and listening to the same thing over and over again. It will bring you no profit to declare the word if you don't have faith for it in your heart and believe that what you said will come to pass! The enemy loves when we waste time pronouncing and speaking things from the Word of God that we don't even believe is so! What we are saying may sound good, but it won't produce results if it's not spoken in faith. Faith comes by hearing (Rom. 10:17). Repetition in our hearing of the Word is of great significance. It is by repetitious hearing that our children learn their names, the alphabet, and their home address and telephone number. The more they hear the same thing, the more likely and easier it is for them to remember and respond effortlessly when asked questions. Whatever you hear the most is what you will have faith in! Whatever you focus on will expand.

John 15:7 lets us know that when we abide in Christ and His word abides or takes up residence in us, we can ask what we will and it shall be done for us. We have to abide in Christ through abiding in the word. The latter part of verse 23 of Mark 11 says, "and believes that those things which he says will come to pass, he will have whatsoever he says." When you and I live in agreement with the word, declare it in faith, and operate in the necessary corresponding actions, we will receive the same victorious results that our savior did as He walked on the earth! Let's start setting time aside every day to hear the word of God. Get and listen to CDs and DVDs of teachings by your Pastor or other anointed bible teachers. We should listen multiple times daily because once is not enough for the word to impregnate your spirit. God has a proven track record of success! Let's agree with Him by coming into agreement with His word!

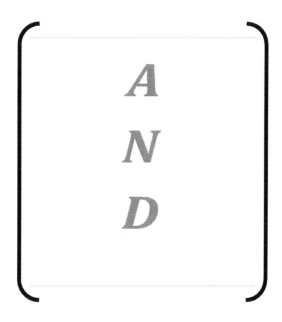

> **Mark 11:23** "For truly I say to you, That whoever shall say to this mountain, Be you removed, and be you cast into the sea; and shall not doubt in his heart, but shall believe that those things which he said shall come to pass; he shall have whatever he said." (AKJV)

3

Understanding Your Role and Responsibility

We have been made speaking spirits just like God. Let me remind you of the Word in Genesis 1:26 that says we were created in God's image and His likeness. Paul said "as He is, so are we in this world" (I John 4:17). When you and I sit back and watch what takes place in the world and in our lives without getting involved, the devil has a field day. We have to arise out of our lazy boy chairs, turn off the television and get busy searching God's Word for answers to the dilemmas we see around us. We must address situations that have gotten out of God's order by speaking the written Word concerning those situations. Then continue seeking the Word to find another scripture that confirms the same principle concerning the matter at hand. Demand, by declaring the Word with authority that things line up according to what you are speaking from the Word! God said in Isaiah 55:11, "So shall my word be that goes forth out of my mouth: it shall not return to me void, but it shall accomplish that which I please, and it shall prosper in the thing whereto I sent it." Begin to thank God daily and give Him the glory in advance for the outcome, the answer to your prayer, as you decreed and declared it to be. Do not take "no" for an answer when the Word says "yes!" Insist, persist, command, demand and declare your prosperity, healing, deliverance, freedom, liberty, restoration and salvation for loved ones NOW! Mark 11:23 says, "For truly I say to you, That whoever shall say to this mountain, Be you removed, and be you cast into the sea; and shall not doubt in his heart, but shall believe that those things which he said shall come to pass; he shall have whatever he said." YOU have to declare it.

Too often believers have neglected their role in their desires coming to pass. As believers, we know and understand that we have to believe God, but it doesn't stop there. The word says in James 2:26 that "faith without works is dead." We cannot believe God for a new job without ever leaving our house or searching the internet to pursue it. We can't believe to get good grades in school but never study. Unfortunately our thinking has been warped in this area. Our believing God must translate into a corresponding action. The action plan we execute will complement how we believe God to change our current situation. Far too long we've sat back waiting on God to change it. We've heard the scripture in Psalm 27:14 that says, "wait on the lord and be of good courage and he will strengthen your heart", but we've taken it out of its proper context; we've parked there prematurely, without receiving the revelation that was intended for our implementation of the principle. The word 'wait' as it is used in this verse of scripture, actually means to stay in a place of expectancy and to be ready and available. If I remain in a place of expectancy, I will also prepare! Prepare for what you may ask. You should be preparing for the thing that you're waiting to take place.

It should flow like this:

1. First you have a desire to do something.

2. You must begin to prepare to do it by gathering information concerning it (such as research, which may include reading and studying, or inquiring about it from someone who has successfully done what you're seeking to accomplish).

3. You will have to apply the necessary steps to go after what you want

Once you have put into action the required work or plan, you will be in a place of expectation for the desired result to come to pass. The process is not yet complete. During consistent implementation of this plan or action, you must declare the promises from the word that secure your success in that area in order not to become weary in the process. Patience will produce the manifestation of your desire. This sums it all up: desire, preparation, implementation, expectation, declaration, patience, manifestation. Oh yeah, we must not forget celebration! As we fulfill our role and responsibility we can have what we want. It will take effort and action on our part, but you know I'm going to ask you this question, how bad do you want it.

> **2 Corinthians 4:18** "While we look not at the things which are seen, but at the things which are not seen: for the things which are seen are temporal; but the things which are not seen are eternal." (AKJV)

4

Change Your Focus

*H*ave you ever been on an airplane and had the opportunity to sit in the window seat? Did you notice how small everything on the ground looked as you flew high in the sky? Let me tell you, that's how tiny and minute our circumstances are in the eyes of God and it is the same view we are supposed to have. One of the Hebrew names for God is "El Elyon", meaning He is the most high God. In other words, there is nothing above Him and nobody greater than Him. Nothing and nobody can even compare to the magnitude of His authority and power. We are children of the most high God and He "has raised us up together, and made us sit together in heavenly places in Christ Jesus" (Ephesians 2:6). Therefore, we don't magnify our problems or allow them to overwhelm us. Our situations and life challenges pale in comparison to what Jesus has finished on Calvary's cross for us. Do you realize that every temptation, test, and trial that we will ever face has already been dealt with by Jesus' death, burial, resurrection, and ascension to the right hand of God the Father? The Word says in Isaiah 53:5, "He [Jesus] was wounded for our transgressions, He was bruised for our iniquities: the chastisement of our peace was upon Him; and with His stripes we are healed." Anything that will ever arise to *dis-ease* us, according to Isaiah 53:5, has already been dealt with by our Lord. My pastor says, "Whatever Jesus died for, we were delivered from."

The bible must be the final authority in our lives for everything that comes into our lives. Our focus must change from looking at the natural circumstances of life to looking to the Word of God and what it has to say about the things that confront us. While circumstances may be real, at best they only represent facts. Scripture always goes beyond mere facts to present us with the truth concerning our situation. Biblical truth always triumphs over and surpasses facts. Let's do as instructed by 2 Corinthians 4:18 and not look at the things which are seen because they are temporary and subject to change.

We must also be mindful of what we allow ourselves to look at. Psalms 101:3 says it like this, "I will set no wicked thing before my eyes." What we look at determines what we see. What we see will determine what we focus our attention on. Again, to quote my pastor, "whatever you focus on will expand." If what we are focusing on is good, it will expand and we will have more of it. On the other hand, if what we are focusing on is bad, such as our problems, it will also expand and we will also have more of that. It's so vital that we train ourselves to stop focusing on the problems in our lives and instead find a scripture in the bible that addresses them, allowing the Word to be the focus of our meditation and spoken prayers.

We were created to dream, vision cast, and meditate. Did you know that by dreaming, vision casting, and meditating, you are actually opening yourself to the voice of the Holy Spirit to share, in part, with you some of the things God has for you? The Bible says in 1Corinthians 2:9-10, "But as it is written, eye hath not seen, nor ear heard, neither have entered into the heart of man, the things which God hath prepared for them that love him. But God has revealed them to us by his Spirit: for the Spirit searches all things, yes, the deep things of God." You see, the Holy Spirit, through our dreams, vision casting, and meditating, gives us glimpses of our future so we can begin to give birth to it in prayer as we speak, declare and release our faith for those things to be manifested.

Focusing on the truth of the Word will keep us from being distracted by the facts of our situations. Focusing on the Word will redirect our thoughts towards a solution and condition our minds to embrace God's truth, which always supersedes the natural facts of our current reality. Focusing on the Word will strengthen our faith, open our heart to hear from the Spirit of God, and expand our capacity to receive what we need from the Lord. The light of the Word will fill us with truth and bring us victory.

Romans 12:2 "And be not conformed to this world: but be you transformed by the renewing of your mind, that you may prove what is that good, and acceptable, and perfect, will of God." (AKJV)

5

Flip the Script

*W*e must stay on course and follow God's principles in order to reach our full potential in Him. It starts with being full of His Word. We cannot speak confidently if the Word is not abundantly in us. Out of the abundance of the heart, the mouth will speak. We must spend time hearing, reading, studying and meditating on what God has said and not clichés and quotes that we have heard from others. Those sayings have very limited benefit, but the Word will always produce fruit and stand the test of time; because God's word is established forever (Psalms 119:89). The Word won't fail. In Matthew 5:18God says, "For truly I say to you, Till heaven and earth pass, one stroke or one pronunciation mark shall in no wise pass from the law, till all be fulfilled." Wow! What a covenant! We can rest upon His promises. That's right, take the load off and cast all of your cares upon Him because He cares for you!

We must retrain ourselves and develop the habit of speaking God's Word. Do you say what you see, or what you want to see? For example, when something doesn't go right during your day, instead of saying, "if it's not one thing, it's another," say, "thanks be to God, which gives [me] the victory through [my] Lord Jesus Christ" (I Corinthians 15:57). When you are not feeling well, instead of saying, "This pain is killing me," say, "By His stripes I am healed, despite how I feel" (Isaiah 53:5). This is going to take some practice because you've probably become accustomed to saying what you see or how you feel. Using the scriptures to train yourself to say what you want to see is called renewing your mind. As you begin renewing your mind, you'll begin to break free from thought patterns and mindsets that are so common to the world's belief system. That's a good thing because you'll speak differently, act differently and have different results. People will begin to take note of your life and want the peace, prosperity, and joy that you have. This is the way it should be. We're not supposed to blend in and conform to the world's belief system and manner of living. We are to stand out. Didn't the Word call us the salt of the earth and the light of the world (Matthew 5:13-14)? Salt doesn't blend in to food; it brings the flavor of the food out. If you put a lot of salt on what you are about to eat, it will take over and you won't taste the food, only the salt. Likewise, light does not blend with darkness; it takes over and totally overcomes darkness. We have been called by God to stand out and take over in the earth, not blend in! Flip the script and begin saying what you want to see. Declare the Word of God in and over every negative situation you encounter.

DECLARE

> **2Timothy 1:7** "For God has not given us the spirit of fear; but of power, and of love, and of a sound mind." (AKJV)

6

*R*efuse to Fear

Don't allow fear of the unknown or fear of what is known to grip you. Always remember that every gloomy or negative (evil) report you could ever be given is subject to change. Never meditate on the bad things you see or the negative reports you hear. Doing so only produces fear which according to 1 John 4:18, involves torment. Torment causes mental suffering, pain, agony, misery and a host of other negative effects. It's vital that you learn to renounce the spirit of fear so you can escape its torment. Otherwise, fear will smother your ambitions, kill your dreams, rob you of hope, void your faith and destroy your future. "For God has not given us a spirit of fear, but of power, love, and of a sound mind" (2 Timothy 1:7).

Fear and faith cannot coincide with each

another. You cannot be fearful about something and at the same time operate in faith concerning it. Once fear grips your mind, it will block your meditation of the Word. The only thing that you'll be able to see is the problem and not the bible's promise. Without meditating on the Word, you won't have the information, insight, and inspiration necessary to speak the written Word with power and authority to cause a change in your situation. It is meditating on what God has said that will paint a new picture on the canvas of your mind, allowing you to see something different and speak in such a way that a favorable outcome is assured for your life. See yourself with the victory, speaking it and claiming it as your own. Be determined to walk by faith and not by sight as instructed by 2 Corinthians 5:7. Trust the Word of God. He cannot lie! Numbers 23:19 says, "God is not a man that He should lie, neither the son of man that He would have to repent." Mark 11:22 says, "Have faith in God." Resist fear (False Evidence Appearing Real) and believe the report of the Lord.

Make a decision now to destroy your fears by fighting the good fight of faith. When a fearful thought enters your mind, immediately you have a decision to make. You're going to either reject and cast down that thought, or think on, and consider and accept that thought. In 2 Corinthians 10:5 the word says "to cast down every imagination that exalts itself against the knowledge of God and bring into captivity every thought to the obedience of Christ". To cast something is to throw it in a quick swift motion. This is what you must do with the thought, quickly throw it out. Secondly, replace that lie with the truth of God's word. For example if a thought should come that says "you will never get out of this situation", you cast that negative thought down by saying, "I rebuke that lie in Jesus' name. In every situation I am more than a conqueror. I can do all things through Christ that strengthens me; I always win!" Declare the word in faith, and set yourself to do this more than one time.

The battlefield is in the mind. Satan will attempt to harass you throughout the day, by bombarding your mind with thoughts of fear and defeat. The enemy is strategic and very persistent. That is why you must be strategic, consistent and persistent! We know he's coming, so let's take an offensive posture, and have a plan already in place! Keep rejecting his thoughts of worry, fear and failure, and continue to declare the word over and over!

Thirdly, find at least three scriptures that promise you victory in the specific area of fear that you face. One scripture is not enough to substantiate the case of evidence you are building in your spirit in order to ward off the enemy's assaults. You can't be lazy with this! Everyday go over those scriptures until they become a part of you. The bible says, "When the enemy comes in like a flood, the spirit of the Lord will lift up a standard against him." Well, what's the standard that the Holy Spirit will lift up? It is the word that you have put into yourself to counteract the lies of the enemy! As I have said before, no word in, no word out!

The scripture says "looking unto Jesus the author and finisher of our faith". Jesus is always our great example setter. When he was tempted by Satan to stray from the word, He replied to every thought and temptation by boldly declaring 'it is written!' You too must be full of what has been written about your situation. What you hear in abundance is what you will have faith for! Let's keep the word in us in abundance, so that the abundance of the word we possess will drown out Satan's habitual lies. Notice that I said stay 'full'. How far can you go on a quarter of gas in your tank? Not very far; am I correct? You must refuse to allow the spirit of fear to harass you any longer. The enemy's desire is to back you up from aggressively pursuing and receiving the promises of God. His ultimate desire is to prevent you from fulfilling your preordained purpose and reaching your God ordained destiny. Refuse to fear! Get back in the driver's seat! Next stop, your destiny! Here are a few scriptures that I use daily to keep fear under my feet: *Psalm 91, Isaiah 41:10, Psalm 23, Philippians 4:8.* Make these scriptures apart of your morning or daily fellowship time with the Lord, and watch fear take flight away from your presence!

> **2 Corinthians 10:5** "Casting down imaginations, and every high thing that exalts itself against the knowledge of God, and bringing into captivity every thought to the obedience of Christ." (AKJV)
>
> **Proverbs 18:21** "Death and life are in the power of the tongue: and they that love it shall eat the fruit thereof." (AKJV)

7

Right Thinking, Right Speaking

*I*n order to speak correctly you must think correctly. What types of thoughts dominate your thought life? Are they words of doubt and unbelief concerning the promises of God? How about negative words that may have been spoken to you or an evil report that you've just heard? It is amazing how we can rehearse a negative word or thought in our minds and develop enough faith to believe that those bad things just might come to pass? Well, faith works that same way if we would just flip the script and began to rehearse over and over in our thoughts what God has said to us. If we did so, we would receive faith to believe that His promises will come to pass.

It is so important that we monitor our thoughts and correct the ones that are contrary to the Word. Thoughts that are unattended and not dealt with will take root and become difficult to uproot even when new, correct information is introduced. That is why it says in 2 Corinthians 10:5, "Casting down imaginations, and every high thing that exalts itself against the knowledge of God, and bringing into captivity every thought to the obedience of Christ."

Let's break down 2 Corinthians 10:5 so we can get an understanding of the verse. To cast down means to throw away. A fisherman does this as he casts his pole into the water; it's a swift quick motion. We must quickly and swiftly get rid of any thought that does not agree with what God has said. It generally starts in our imagination. We can imagine some crazy stuff at times. However, our imagination was given to us by God. It's a resource given to everyone to help plan, think, believe, explore and form mental pictures of things not currently experienced through the natural physical senses. When we use our imaginations the way God intended we become empowered to live life without boundaries. To use our imagination to entertain misfortune and unhappy scenarios is a strategy from the devil to counter God's original plan and purpose for meditating.

The Word in 2 Corinthians 2:5 also says to

cast down every high thing that exalts itself against the knowledge of God. What are high things? These are things that have weight or factual proof in the natural physical realm. A high thing could be a positive x-ray or MRI, a zero checking account balance, poor credit rating, or disobedient children. Regardless of how much proof or evidence a high thing has, when we allow our imagination to connect with a scriptural promise, it ignites our faith and enables us, when we declare the Word, to pull the promises of God out of the spiritual realm into the natural physical realm. We don't look at the things that can be seen with our natural eyes because those things are only an indicator of the physical realm. Instead, we see with the eyes of faith those things that exist in the realm of the spirit; natural things are subject to change but that which is spiritual is eternal (2 Corinthians 4:18). Therefore we look to God's word for proof of existence concerning what we desire and not our situation or circumstance which is subject to change.

Did you know that when you declare God's Word over your thoughts in spite of what you see, you bring your thoughts into captivity (subjection) to the obedience of Christ? Pay close attention to what you are speaking. Psalms 141:39(NIV) says "Set a guard over my mouth O Lord; keep watch over the doors of my lips"; Psalms 119:11 says, "Your Word I have hid in my heart that I might not sin against you." Will we be judged by the words we speak? Yes. Matthew 12:36 tells us that we will. "But I say to you, that every idle word that men shall speak, they shall give account thereof in the day of judgment." The word idle means inactive, unemployed, meaningless, and frivolous. The words we speak must have a meaningful assignment which declaring the Word provides.

Whatever we hear in abundance will absolutely affect our thinking, and what affects our thinking will absolutely affect the words that flow out of our mouths. What we speak impacts the quality of our lives. Proverbs 18:21 says, "Death and life are in the power of the tongue: and they that love it shall eat the fruit thereof." This is why hearing and speaking the wrong information, such as what is seen instead of what you want to see is so detrimental. Guard your ears and take heed to what and how you hear as exhorted by Luke in Luke 8:18.

Reaching our expected or desired end is up to us and not God. He said in Jeremiah 29:11, "For I know the thoughts that I think toward you, says the Lord, thoughts of peace and not of evil, to give you a future and a hope." God's plan is that we live a good life! We have to make choices to embrace his plans (thoughts) towards us. Have you ever had plans for your children to get great grades, graduate, attend college and have a successful career? Sometimes they get side-tracked and make some bad choices even though you had all of these wonderful plans for them. Ultimately, despite your plans and desires for your children, particularly as they grow up, the decisions are up to them to make. They must choose the good life. Likewise, as the children of God, we have to get back into the driver's seat and secure our destiny. We have to take control of what we will be, do and have in life. Let's decide once and for all to agree with God and declare His Word daily over all of our affairs! Let us let God arise and His enemies be scattered!

> **Proverbs 28:1** "...but the righteous are bold as a lion."
> (AKJV)

8

Be Bold As a Lion

As previously stated, we must not only read the Word of God, we must study and meditate on it. This will help us to become so full of the Word that when situations and circumstances come in our lives to challenge and distract us, the Word in us will instantly and boldly arise out of us to assist us to deal with the challenge. Spiritual boldness comes from having a confident relationship with the Lord and faith in His Word. Getting there requires a desire for Him apart from anything He can do for you, along with regular disciplined study of His Word to reprogram your thinking.

Being bold in prayer will have you declaring what God said in the face of the enemy as well as those who will think you are in denial about the facts surrounding your condition or situation. It took boldness for Jesus to go into seemingly hopeless situations and speak life and command change. The bible has many examples of this. One such example is found in John 11:1-46. Three days after Lazarus died Jesus stood outside of the tomb and called him forth (from the dead), and Lazarus came. Another example is when Jairus' daughter died. Jesus came to her house and called her to awaken after she had been pronounced dead (Mark 5:21-24, 35-42). In both of these examples, the words that Jesus spoke were filled with resurrection power.

Jesus told the man with the withered hand to stretch forth his hand and he did; his hand was restored (Mark 3:5). He told the ten lepers to go see the priest, and as they went, they were cleansed (Luke 17:14). These examples reveal that Jesus' words were filled with healing power.

Recall that Jesus said at the tomb of Lazarus, "Father, I thank you that You have heard Me." He said it aloud so the people could hear Him. There are times when we will have to declare the Word aloud so people will hear and see the glory of God. What Jesus did in each of these situations was declare the will of God over the facts that were present and evident. Jesus knew that what He said was seemingly absurd and unrealistic to the natural eyes and ears of those who heard His words and witnessed the scene. He both looked and sounded strange to them. Yet, He had so much faith in His Father fulfilling the words He spoke that He was able to boldly declare aloud for everyone to hear. He knew that just as they heard, they would also see the glory of God. Here's a lesson: neither concern yourself with nor consider the doubters and naysayers who will come across your path and offer their so called "expert" advice. As a born again believer, the Word is where you gather expert opinion, advice, and principles necessary to live victoriously. So get in the Word and find out what it has to say about your situation. Begin to study and meditate on the scriptures. Repeatedly go over them, write them down, and post them somewhere where you'll be sure to regularly see them. Keep the Word before you daily until you are fully convinced that what God has said is the truth and it is the final Word concerning your condition or situation. Release the Word by declaring it aloud every day until what you are speaking comes to pass. The righteous are as bold as lions. Boldly declare what God has said!

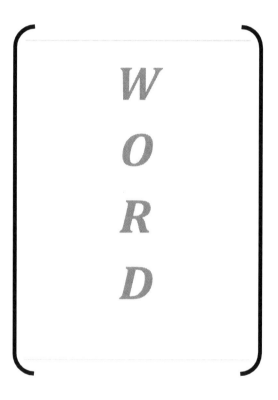

> **John 8:31** "Then said Jesus to the Jews which believed on him, If you continue in my word, then are you my disciples indeed." (AKJV)

9

Consistency Is the Key

We must be consistent in our study of the Word, believing, praying and speaking our dreams that line up with the promises of God. We cannot speak something from the Word today and then tomorrow speak things that express doubt and unbelief. Consistency is the key to breakthrough. I have found that often it is not that we do not do the right things, because most Christians do the right things (at least as it pertains to spiritual matters), it's just that we do not do them long enough to get the results that the Word has promised. If we are being challenged in a certain area, say for instance our health, it is imperative that we remain consistent speaking our declarations of faith. Too often, we start a faith project without all of the proper materials. We take off running without putting the correct amount of Word "fuel" in our "tank." Here's a question, how long is a plane going to remain in flight without the proper amount of fuel for its journey? Not long, that's for sure. Likewise, we won't be able to go the full journey to receive the end of our faith (manifestation) if we have not put in enough of the Word to help sustain us and keep us on course over time. The pathway to destiny and having our dreams fulfilled is not a one shot deal or necessarily a quick and easy journey. It is going to require that we be consistent and persistent in studying, believing, praying and speaking the Word, regardless of what we see, until what we see is what we have been speaking by faith! Consistency enables us to use time to our advantage as we pursue our dreams and ultimately our destiny. Being consistent to the process that faith requires will turn time into an ally instead of an enemy that causes discouragement.

Being consistent also helps us in times of adversity. Jesus was on a ship with his disciples and a storm arose. While the disciples were panicking, Jesus was asleep. Why? Because He had already spoken the Word, "Let us go to the other side."

Luke 8:22-25:
v.22 Now it came to pass on one of those days, that he entered into a boat, himself and his disciples; and he said unto them, Let us go over unto the other side of the lake: and they launched forth.
v. 23 But as they sailed he fell asleep: and there came down a storm of wind on the lake; and they were filling [with water], and were in jeopardy.
v. 24 And they came to him, and awoke him, saying, Master, master, we perish. And he awoke, and

rebuked the wind and the raging of the water: and they ceased, and there was a calm.

v. 25 And he said unto them, Where is your faith? And being afraid they marveled, saying one to another, Who then is this, that he commanded even the winds and the water, and they obey him? (ASV)

You and I must do what Jesus did. He arose, spoke boldly and took authority over the storm. They made it to the other side because Jesus had faith in the Word He had spoken.

It is easy to speak 'peace be still' when there is no sign of a storm or challenge on the horizon. When we are in the midst of a difficult situation or a storm, however, can we speak the Word regardless of what we see, hear, or are facing? It is during these times in particular that we must constantly pray and speak the Word. The devil is quite consistent in his attacks against us. He is a thief whose goal, according to John 10:10, is to steal, kill and destroy our lives. He aims to cause us to forfeit and give up in our pursuit of the purpose and plan of God for our lives. He wants to talk us out of our expected end result that God has foreordained and promised. There was a song we sung quite frequently that said, "Whose report will you believe? We shall believe the report of the Lord." This is where we sometime loose it, when a negative or evil report comes our way. Instead of losing it, we must gather ourselves by meditating on the Word, going over and over what God has said about our situation, and continue speaking the Word until what God has said in His Word comes to pass in our life. Don't get weary in the process; Keep the Word in your heart and in your mouth. Consistency is the key to reaping your harvest of blessing!

> **Colossians 3:16** "Let the word of Christ dwell in you richly in all wisdom; teaching and admonishing one another in psalms and hymns and spiritual songs, singing with grace in your hearts to the Lord."

10

Stay Full of the Word

I have learned that whatever you hear in abundance is what you will have faith for. We have to examine and guard what we allow ourselves to hear. That is why I submit myself to hearing the word at least two to three times daily. Now that is not a rule that you must follow. I am simply saying that the word must be a priority in your daily regimen. Some people use the word like a spare tire. They only pull it out in the event of an emergency. Colossians 3:16 says that the word should dwell in us. What does dwell mean? Dwell means to continuously abide in a place. Have you ever had water abide in your drain? It begins to build and starts to rise. If it is not let out it will overflow onto the floor. Well if we let the word dwell and abide in us, we will gain from it because of revelation and understanding; we will begin to rise above limitations and obstacles that present themselves in our lives.

Notice that Colossians 3:16 goes on to say that the word should dwell in us in all wisdom. Wisdom is operational insight or simply how we operate in the knowledge that we have gained. Secondly, notice it says to admonish one another in psalms, hymns and spiritual songs. This means to give out what you have received! Don't just be full of the word and not impart or share what you have received!

Ok, back to the water in the drain analogy. If water dwells in a drain and begins to rise without flowing out or over onto something else, it will become stagnant and begin to stink. It must flow over to something else in order to keep refilling and receiving more. In other words, God always has more than you in mind when He tells you to be full of the word! Many times I'll be asked to pray for something that I may not know much information about. While in prayer it's amazing the amount of the word that will come up in me concerning it; because I have deposited much word in me, Holy Spirit brings up what I need to declare concerning it. The Holy Spirit can only bring back to your remembrance what you've put in or studied. Nothing in, nothing out!

We must boldly declare the word in the face

of all opposition and all distractions. This boldness and confidence comes from revelation of the word. People ask me all the time, how do you pray as boldly as you do? I respond by saying I believe the word! If God said it then I agree with it! This has come as a result of meditating over and over and over again on the word. Listening to CDs; Hearing the same ones over and over until I believe and am totally convinced that the word or promise, not the temporary situation, is the truth. I had to learn to trust God's word, and realize that His promises are written to me personally. I had to believe that He loves me unconditionally and will never fail or forsake me. I had to read daily scriptures like Psalms 91, and Isaiah 41:10. I had to renew my mind in order to believe the word. Then I was able to lean only on God's word for all of my challenges, instead of leaning on my own understanding. According to Proverbs 3:5, the word has to be the final authority in your life! Everything else is questionable, temporary, and subject to change. The word cannot change. It is forever settled. God has exalted His word even above His name! We can stand and depend on His word.

One day Jesus and his disciples were on a boat. When they got on the boat Jesus said, "let us go to the other side"! After He said that, He laid down for a nap. While Jesus was sleeping there arose a great storm. The winds blew fiercely and water quickly entered the boat. The disciples woke

Jesus up and said "don't you care that we are perishing?" Jesus arose and rebuked the wind and the waves by saying, "peace be still!" He then turned to the disciples and said, "How is it that you have no faith?" You see, Jesus had declared the word ahead of time! He expected them to do what He did! All they had to do was agree with what the word had said and declare it.

On the boat, Jesus declared the word when they first set out to go! You've got to declare the word even before you go forth with what you're endeavoring. Of course because you're moving towards your goal or desire a storm will arise. But I'm telling you to be full of the word so that even in the face of a storm, you will arise as Jesus did, with no fear, declare the word, and watch the magnificence of God be demonstrated on your behalf! Let's agree to stay full of the word!

Conclusion: The Take Away

Accepting any and everything that comes your way in life is not how we, as believers, were originally designed to function. We were created to reign, live victorious, and show forth God's glory in the earth. It is my hope that after having read this book, you have embraced this truth and are ready to "shift gears"; I hope you will now decree and declare the Word of God to challenge and contend against the circumstances, situations, and affairs in your life that have been a source of frustration and pain. Change is on the way when you rise up (change your posture and position) and begin to decree and declare what God has already said in His word.

If you do not boldly declare the Word over your present condition and situation, your present condition and situation will boldly declare to you that you are defeated. Don't be guilty of having a lot of information but not being the better because of it. There is now more information available to us than ever before. We have T.V, radio, the internet, CDs, DVDs, books and more. We have anointed ministry gifts that are teaching and preaching the Word and making it simple for us to apply to our lives. Yet there are still too many Christians struggling and not experiencing the victorious life in Christ. What is missing? The missing element is the fulfillment of our role and responsibility which   not only includes obedience to God's Word but also declaring God's Word in faith. Say what He says and your environment and life will conform to the spoken Word of God!

Jump Start Declarations

Declaration for Daily Winning

I decree and declare that out of my belly flow rivers of living waters and nothing around me can remain dead because of the life that flows from me.

I decree and declare that I am empowered to prosper and created to win. I am full of creativity and witty ideas which enable my success and prosperity. The favor of God is upon my life and my endeavors are blessed. What I put my hands to always succeeds.

I declare that I will never be comfortable with "average" or the status quo. I live by faith. I decree the Spirit of the Lord has equipped me for the extraordinary and to produce uncommon results in Jesus' name.

I decree and declare that all of my needs are met. I am rich and not poor; the lender and not the borrower. Wealth and riches are in my houses and that which attempts to devour my sustenance is rebuked. Every financial seed that I have sown in the kingdom of God will produce a harvest after its own kind. I am destined to finance kingdom projects. I profess that I am fulfilled in my life's purpose and the assignments God has ordained for me.

I decree and declare that I am fruitful and I multiply righteousness in the earth. I am a faithful steward and God can count on me. I am an example of a believer, a great soul winner for Christ, and a disciple maker. My pastor can also count on me to assist him/her in carrying out the ministry's vision. Whatsoever my hands find to do in support of the ministry, I do it with all my might to the glory of God. I have been called into the kingdom of God for such a time as this.

I declare that I serve the Lord with gladness and come before His presence with singing. It delights me to serve others and I decree that I am a great blessing to my church and pastor. The compassionate heart of Jesus flows through me and love is my motivation for serving my pastor and church family. I decree that as He (Christ) is so am I in the earth. In Jesus' name, it is so!

Declaration for Family & Marriage Life

I decree and declare that my marriage glorifies Christ Jesus! As a husband, I love my wife even as Christ loves the church and I treat her as a treasure [As a wife, I love my husband and treat him with respect and honor]. My husband/wife's heart safely trusts in me and the bonds of our marital unity are strengthened daily. We work through difficult situations together and divorce is never an option!

I decree and declare that every generational curse is broken off my marriage and family and we are released to live in generational blessings! Anything that tries to alienate, frustrate, and separate us from each other is exposed, rejected, and made null and void…it will not work! No weapon formed against my marriage and family will prosper.

I decree and declare that we love one another generously, we easily forgive each other, and affirm the uniqueness we each posses. Our house is filled with peace and is a place where angels abide and the presence of God resides. Joy and laughter fills the environment of our home and we enjoy spending time together as a family.

I decree and declare that my marriage and family life is satisfying and fulfilling. My spouse and children are a blessing to me and they infuse my life with love. I speak these blessing over my family and marriage in Jesus' name.

Declaration to Proclaim Over Children

In the name of Jesus, I decree and declare that my seed is delivered from the devices, trickery, and schemes of dark forces and evil, wicked individuals. My sons and daughters will not be held captive, enslaved, or in bondage to lies, deceit, addictions, appetites or generational failures and weaknesses. No! They will be saved, delivered, taught of the Lord and great will be their peace and prosperity in Jesus' name.

I decree and declare that my children will be nourished at my side and instructed in the ways of Godliness. They will become instruments of righteousness. Yes, they will walk in truth and their days will be fulfilled. Mighty men and great women they are destined to become for Your glory and the gates of hell will not prevail against them.

I decree and declare that sickness and disease will be far from my children and they will enjoy good health and long life. My children will be good stewards of their bodies. They will eat and drink foods that promote a sound body and mind. No illegal substance will enter their bodies.

I decree that spouses are being prepared for my children even now and they will not be unequally yoked. Their mates will be holy and set apart unto God.

As their parent, my children can   pattern themselves after me and follow me as I follow Christ. These things are so in Jesus' name!

Declaration for Making Decisions

In the name of Jesus, I decree and declare that every major decision I make will be based on the principles, patterns, and precepts found in the Word of God. Because I love what God loves and hates what He hates, I seek Him early and often for direction and clarity to keep me in the perfect will of God. Therefore, I decree that wisdom, discernment, and understanding will rest on my head so that I always know the precise course of action to take, the right path to pursue, and the correct option to choose to keep my life on course with destiny and always positioned for blessings.

I decree and declare that my decisions will not be marked by folly and foolishness but rather Spirit and Word of God which leads me into truth. Furthermore, I declare that my ears will only hear the council of Godly men and women and not voices from strange and unfamiliar sources that love not the Lord. I decree and declare that I will eat and enjoy the fruit that is produced in my life as a result of consistently making good decisions and Godly choices. I call for this manifestation now, in Jesus' name.

Declaration for Business/Success

I decree and declare that the vision God has given me will succeed, prosper and profit in the marketplace. Doors of opportunity will open for me and the favor of God rests upon my endeavors. My business efforts are blessed of the Lord, the marketplace embraces the products and services that I bring to her, and men seek me out to transact business with me.

I decree and declare that I have an anointing to do business. This anointing brings me before great men and women who connect me to others which results in the establishment of a profitable financial network for the products and services my company produces.

I decree and declare that because of the manner in which I service my clientele, I am blessed with a good reputation that brings me repeat customers, new clients, unique marketing venues, and unusual revenue streams that sustain and enlarge my business even in the midst of an economic downturn.

I decree and declare that I am pregnant with much potential and I will overcome every challenge and obstacle to the plan and purpose of God for my life and business! I will fulfill all that God has called me to do and be in the world of commerce. I will bless God's house with the fruit of my financial success. I call it done in Jesus' name.

Declaration for Promotion

In the name of Jesus, I decree that every border and boundary be removed from my life that is restricting my promotion or limiting my increase. Every obstruction and deterrent to my destiny is removed right now! I decree that every hindering spirit is now bound in Jesus' name! I cannot and I will not fail, for victory is mine perpetually in every situation. Delays are not a denial for me; they work in my favor.

I decree and declare that I am a winner and a champion! I'm above only and never beneath. With Christ, I always triumph. Setbacks are setups for my next promotion. Every test I encounter in life will soon become my testimony that will assist others to overcome!! Father God you will get the glory for the great things you are doing in my life, so I thank you in advance!

Declaring the Word Seed

I decree and declare that every word seed which God has not planted in me is uprooted now and replaced with the Word of God. Every evil word spoken against God's purpose and plan for my life will not grow, flourish, bear fruit or come to pass. I command it to be uprooted and brought to naught.

I decree and declare that the Word of God is a flourishing seed in my life. It is my daily meditation and source of inspiration that draws the spirit of wisdom, revelation, truth and understanding to my life. Because of the word seed, I do not walk in darkness, but in the marvelous light. The Word is a lamp to my feet and a light for my pathway causing me to see all things clearly. Every word God has spoken to me will surely come to pass! Though the vision may tarry, I will wait expectantly for it and in the fullness of time, I decree that I will possess it, and it will be mine to the glory of God.

Furthermore, I decree and declare that the words of my mouth and the mediation of my heart are acceptable unto the Lord. The words that I speak will minister grace and healing to those who hear them.

Father, your word declares that death and life are in the power of the tongue. I release life over myself, my family, my church, my community, and every situation or circumstance that I will ever face. I choose to speak life and declare Your word and not the problem. You will create the fruit of my lips. My mouth shall utter good things. Your word declares that a word spoken in due season is like apples of gold in settings of silver. I now provide You the access You deserve to move in the affairs of Your creation by the faith filled words of my mouth! Let Your will be done in the earth as it is in heaven! I agree with Your will and Your plans. Let it come to pass even as You have spoken it. I will give voice to Your word forever, in Jesus' name.

~AMEN

ARISE AND DECLARE YOUR WORD

JOURNAL

Deborah L. Grant

84

Deborah L. Grant

Deborah L. Grant

About the Author

Deborah Grant is an author, servant leader, and teacher.

This anointed woman of God is on fire as she passionately promotes the kingdom of God!" Arise and Declare the Word" is Deborah's second published book. Her first book, entitled "Have You Prayed for Your Pastor Lately?" has empowered the body of Christ by practical instruction on how to lift up their senior pastors and leaders in prayer. Deborah has written specific prayers throughout the book concerning pastors' visions and assignments. With a desire to pour into others the wisdom and revelation that she has received over the years, book number three is forthcoming.

Deborah has been married for 20 years to Elder Donald Grant and is a proud mother of three beautiful children: Jada, Donovan and Nia. Since its inception, Deborah has been a partner of Spirit of Faith Christian Center, under the leadership of Drs'. Mike and Dee Dee Freeman. She serves on the Ministerial Staff and is the Director of Intercessory Prayer, both for over 20 years. She is also an instructor at Spirit of Faith Bible institute.

Deborah's whole-heart's desire is teach and develop people to have an intimate, beneficial relationship with God, through the study of the word and prayer.